Albert Zabriskie Gray

Jesus Only

And other Sacred Songs

Albert Zabriskie Gray

Jesus Only
And other Sacred Songs

ISBN/EAN: 9783337265328

Printed in Europe, USA, Canada, Australia, Japan

Cover: Foto ©Lupo / pixelio.de

More available books at **www.hansebooks.com**

"TO THE PRAISE
OF
His Glory!"

———

"JESUS ONLY; JESUS ALWAYS;
ALL FOR JESUS!"

CONTENTS.

PAGE.

JESUS ONLY.
"Jesus Only!" 7
"The Day is Thine and the Night is Thine!" . 8
He loves me! 9
He can—He will—He does! 10
"Looking unto Jesus." 11
"I stand at the Door and knock," . . . 13
No "Almost!" 15
Follow Jesus! 17
Rest. 19
"Let not your heart be troubled!" . . . 20
"If Thou knewest!" 21
"The Light of the Morning." 23
"Jesus wept." 26
"He giveth His Beloved Sleep." . . . 27

THE CHURCH.
"Jerusalem—the Mother of us all!" . . . 28
The Saviour and the Ship. 30

EUCHARISTIC.
"Lord, evermore give us this Bread!" . . 31
Eucharistic Prayer. 32

ADVENT.
Come, Master, come! 33
An Advent Thought. 35
Waiting! 37

CHRISTMAS.
Hail, Holy Night! 39
O Gates of Glory far above! 41

FEAST OF THE CIRCUMCISION.
"Thou shalt call His Name Jesus!" . . . 43

LENT.
We need to Fast. 44
"Watch and Pray!" 46
A Lenten Thought in Rhyme. 47

PALM SUNDAY.
The Palm beside the Cross. 50

GOOD FRIDAY.
"Lord, have mercy upon us!" 52
"Father, forgive them!" 53

EASTER.
	PAGE.
"He is Risen!"	54
"Lift up your Heads!"	55
"The Resurrection and the Life!"	56

WHIT-SUNDAY.
O Loving Spirit of our God!	57

THE HOLY MARTYRS.
The Holy Innocents.	58
The Army of the Lord.	59

THE CHURCH'S MINISTRY.
"The Noble Army of Martyrs."	60
The Priests of the Most High God.	64

THE CHURCH'S WORK.
"Give!"	66
"Where hast thou gleaned to-day?"	67
Love's Labour.	69
"Why stand ye here all the day idle?"	70
"Labourers together with God."	72
No Time to lose!	73
A Final Question?	73

MISCELLANEOUS.
Shadows.	74
"Thou Sendest Rain."	76
The Parish Church.	78
Science and Faith.	79
Charles Kingsley.	81
"Only another Reverse!"	84
President Garfield.	86
On a Birthday.	87
Farewell!	88
The Wreck of "The Atlantic."	90
In Camp.	94
"Domine, Quo Vadis?"	97
A Christmas Ballad.	101
A Centennial Hymn.	102
"The Crescent and the Cross."	104
A. N.	108
Egypt.	110
Memories.	111

PREFACE.

THESE verses, written, many of them, in the intervals of a Country Rector's busy life and often on the impulse of a sermon ending, are published with no pretension beyond the humble hope that they may, now and then, bring a mite of sacred suggestion or consolation to some struggling or stricken heart—to the life that will hail anything, which helps it in any degree out of its weary self into the higher and sweeter realms of fancy and faith!

A. Z. G.

St. Philip's in the Highlands,
    EASTERTIDE, 1882.

JESUS ONLY.

Jesus Only!

JESUS only! Jesus ever!
  What shall from the Saviour sever!
Heart and hands and life and love
Lifted up to Christ above!

Jesus only! Jesus ever!
O these erring eyes shall never
Find the burden of their loss,
Till they rest—upon His Cross!

Jesus only! Jesus ever!
Pardon, peace and rest forever,
May Thy children find this day,
Lord, as round Thy Cross they pray!

And O at last may they behold,
'Mid the Courts of glittering gold,
In His raiment ever white—
Him the King of Love and Light!

Jesus only! Jesus ever!
Lord, be this my heart's endeavour,
Lifting up mine eyes, to see
" Jesus only "—only Thee!

"The Day is Thine and the Night is Thine!"

MORNING.

HAST seen the golden Daybreak,
   As it climbs above the hill?
So shines the face of Jesus
   To them that do His will!

NOON.

Hast felt the Midday glory
   Of the sweet, soft summer swoon?
So rest thyself in Jesus,
   When comes the burd'ning noon!

EVENING.

Hast marked the Evening shadows,
   As they creep across the sky?
Then raise thy soul to Jesus,
   And find Him ever nigh!

MIDNIGHT.

Hast waked and shuddered sometimes
   In the dark, lone middle-night;
Lift up thy heart to Jesus,
   And He shall be thy Light!

He Loves Me!

HE loved me; in His love He led me;
  He leads me, and His leading is my life:
He lives, and I in Him forever—
He—the Victor for my spirit in the strife!

He sought me—long before I saw Him;
He found me, and His finding was my Grace;
O on the weary, winding pathway,
I am safe with but the gleaming of His Face!

He knows me—Christ my Master knows me;
He pities His poor servant in the dust;
He taketh on Himself my burden,
And that taking of His Love is all my trust.

He loves me—my Redeemer loves me;
And O! what though my spirit sometimes faints,
If Jesus is its own forever,
He—the Life and Love and Labour of His Saints!

He can—He will—He does!

He can; He will; He does!
    He hears; He heeds; He heals
The head, the heart, the life,
    That loves, believes and kneels!

He lives; He loves; He stays
    The longing soul with bread:
His Blood shall wash thee clean,
    Thy heart, thy hands, thy head!

He was; He is; He shall
    In Glory come again:
O watch and pray and wait,
    For no man knoweth when!

Above, below, within—
    O Brother may it be,
The God of Love hath found
    A home, a Throne in thee!

"Looking unto Jesus."

LOOK only to Jesus; look ever and live!
  For to him that looketh Himself He doth give,
In grace and in glory, in love and in life,
In pardon from sin and in rest from the strife.

Be looking to Jesus, by day and by night,
As men in the darkness are looking for light,
Thy Dawn and Thy Noonday—to them that believe
The Glow of the morn and the Dew of the eve!

Be looking to Jesus, O blinded by sin,
Look unto thy Saviour and find Him within!
The cleansing from Heaven that laveth thy brow,
And the Manna from Heaven that satisfies now!

O look unto Jesus! O look while ye may,
Ye sinning and sad in the light of His day!
He once came to save all—He came to save thee,
Thy King in His beauty, thy King on the Tree!

O look unto Jesus! O look to His Cross,
Where all thou hast gainéd will seem but thy loss!
The Crown of His glory a circlet of thorn—
Thy sins thine own Saviour have piercéd and torn!

Be looking to Jesus, O ye who would live,
In the blessing and grace He only can give!
Who long for a love that but He can bestow,
O look unto Jesus, if love ye would know!

O look unto Jesus! O look while ye may,
For the shadows are gathering over the day,
And He, our Redeemer, Transfigured, most Bright
Shall stand in the darkness—the World's only Light!

"I Stand at the Door and Knock."

ART thou in darkness?
    He is the Light!
Hast suffered wrong?
    He is the Right!

Hast thou all squandered?
    He hath all won:
And hast thou wandered?
    He leadeth on.

Art thou so hungry?
    He is thy Food:
And hast thou nothing?
    He is all good.

Art sore and sickened?
    He healeth all.
Hast no one to love?
    He loveth all.

Wouldst thou find labour?
    This is His land:
And askest thou where?
    On every hand.

Art thou so weary?
  He is thy rest.
Art thou so longing?
  In Him be blest.

Art only fearful,
  And full of sin?
He standeth, knocketh!
  Wilt let Him in?

No "Almost!"

"Then Agrippa said unto Paul, 'almost thou persuadest me to be a Christian!'"—Acts xxvi: v. 28.

THERE is no *almost* in this world of love;
All things are perfect from the Throne above:
Thine is a full salvation—full and free ;
Christ Jesus died for all—He died for thee !

Thou mayest not trifle ! Time is brief, and near
The day of Judgment and the hour of fear ;
When prince and peasant, high and low shall stand
Before the Crowned King of every land !

What wilt thou say in such an hour as this !
Where then the doubter's sneer, the traitor's kiss !
O Jesu, when Thou comest in Thy Might,
Where shall Thy foes find refuge from the Light !

O paltry web of poor excuse, wherein
Man wraps himself to sleep of selfish sin—
The "if," the "almost," the "convenient time"—
O shrivelling web before that wrath sublime !

And yet 'tis Love that would invite, persuade—
The love of Him, Who all "our Peace" was
    made;
Who crieth unto you once more to-day,
" Come, at My Feet your heavy burdens lay ! "

I will refresh, will satisfy and bless,
If ye My Saving Name will but confess ;
I gave up Holy Heaven itself for thee,
And all I ask is, "rise and follow Me !"

And I will lead thee to the pastures green,
To waters sweet and of such glorious sheen,
Where Heaven's golden-gated ramparts rise—
My many-mansioned House of Paradise.

No tears, no toil, no tempting trials there!
All sorrows lost in bliss beyond compare !
There shalt thou meet the loved, the gone-
    before,
One Lord, one Life, one Love forevermore !

Follow Jesus!

FOLLOW Jesus! His footprints are still on the way,
'Tis His love that hath made them as plain as the day;
Yes! not even the multitudes following Him,
Hath made them for thee or for any one dim!

Follow Him in His wanderings weary and worn—
Into this were His followers with Him once born!
Follow Him to His Cross — to His cruelest shame,
To this wast thou sealed in the day of thy name!

Follow Jesus! the pathways of earth are not long;
Never one was so weary that found not its song—
The song of the story of the Love that came down
To carry our sorrows—to weave us a Crown!

Follow Him! thou shalt find Him, forever before,
Just before—they shall see Him, who kneel to adore!
The soul, that to Jesus would be looking for life,
Shall find Him, its Captain, in thick of earth's strife!

O to what shall we cling, which He bids us to leave!
With Him as our Leader, to what else shall we cleave!
The way may be darksome and the end may be far,
But the Sun shines to them, who followed His Star!

Follow Him! O arise, my poor soul and leave all!
It is thy Beloved—it is Love that doth call!
In its accents of grace is the peace of the skies;
O who to His call will refuse to arise!

Rest.

REST for the weary—rest
    Forevermore !
To rest with Him, Who all
    Our burdens bore !

Rest from His Blessed Hands,
    That for us toiled,
And healed and helped and held
    The sick and soiled.

Rest at His Feet, and from
    His Holy Side—
The Piercéd Love that once
    For sinners died !

Rest—rest in Jesus—O
    How sweet to rest,
Trembling with labour done,
    Upon His Breast !

Lord, may we rest in Thee !
    As Thou at last,
Thy work and struggle o'er
    And Passion past,

Didst rise by Love's own might
    Unto Thy Throne—
Master, make me to rest
    Amid Thine own !

"Let not your heart be troubled!"

LET not your heart be troubled—come to Me!
Ye look for God to help and I am He!
He that believeth shall be ever blest;
Come unto Me and I will give you rest!

It is a way of tears I too have trod—
I Child of Man and only Son of God!
Its every bitterness I too have known—
For it, for thee, for all I left My Throne!

Yes! every pang and every pain and woe,
And every sob of every love below—
I felt them all; I bore them on My Cross;
They nailed Me fast—they were my love, my loss!

Let not your heart be troubled; come to Me!
I lived; I loved; I died to set you free—
From every care and every grief and woe,
O, were it not, I would have told you so!

"If Thou Knewest!"

O IF thou knewest, knewest, Sinner, how
    He loved thee;
If thou wouldst but seek the beauty of His
    grace;
If thou wouldst but learn how much for thee
    He longeth—
If thou wouldst but long thyself to see His
    Face!

O what for thee hath not thy Saviour done, my
    Brother!
    O what more could He have done of sweetest
        love!
O where wilt thou e'er find a happier portion
    Than He hath for His Beloved prepared
        above!

O if thou knewest, knewest, Sinner, what He
    giveth,
Giveth freely to the doer of His will;
If thou knewest how that yielding all to Jesus,
Is possessing all that is worth keeping still!

O if thou knewest, knewest, thou that living,
    lovest,
  How He is the perfect Glory of all Love!
How that they who live and love in Jesus only,
  Walk already in the Light of Heaven above!

O if thou knewest, knewest, Child of God—the
    Saviour,
  All the blessedness of them who have not
    seen,
Yet have loved, and found fruition of His Glory,
  By the "waters still," amid "the pastures
    green!"

"The Light of the Morning."

"And He shall be as the Light of the Morning, when the sun riseth, even a morning without clouds."
(II Sam. xxiii, v. 4.)

I LOOK and long for the morning
    That follows the night of pain ;
I look for my Master, Jesus,
    Who promised to come again:
I work and I wait in patience,
    For I know His Word is true,
Let never your heart be troubled,
    For I am always with you !

O I know that He is coming—
    The moment it matters not,
If only I am His and He
    Is my Portion and my Lot !
The Heritage of all gladness,
    To fulfil my soul with peace ;
Who shall give me songs for sadness,
    And Holy Heaven's release !

O I love to watch the daylight
    As it creeps above the hill,
For I know it heralds glory,
    Which a weary earth shall thrill !

And though yet the darkness covers,
   And I often feel its sting—
I care not for Jesus cometh,
   With all healing in His wing!

Brighter even than the Angels,
   Which hover about the Throne,
Illumined with the Love that trod
   The wine-press of earth alone;
With a diadem of beauty,
   That pales each radiant star,
And a gleam upon His Visage,
   That lightens my soul from far!

O I know that He is coming,
   By that Light and by that Love,
Streaming all about my pathway
   From the open Gates above—
From the Portals of the Blessed,
   Which He passed for us before,
He, the Conqueror of darkness,
   He, the Saviour evermore!

O! the Glory of that Coming,
   Through those Gates of shining gold,
He, the King of Saints and Angels,
   He, the Same Who came of old!

With the Sceptre of the ages,
   Gleaming in His piercéd Hand,
And His Feet upon the Mountain
   Of His Holy, Blessed Land !*

Master, come unto Thy Kingdom ;
   Make Thy Children in it glad ;
Robe it with the robe of Brightness,
   Which its happy Eden had !
Come, O Jesus, come to bless it ;
   Come to reign amid Thine own ;
Come in Thine eternal glory—
   Master of our hearts alone !

" And His feet shall stand in that day upon the Mount of Olives."—
ZECH. XIV. v. 4.

"Jesus Wept."

BESIDE the grave of love she kneels,
    Her heart upheaved with hope and fear,
Her face of streaming woe upraised,
    As He, Whose Name is Love, draws near!

He stands and weeps—the patient heart,
    Which bore a world of grief alone,
Sheds tears of sweetest sympathy,
    Then bids them roll away the stone.

The dead came forth, the loved returns,
    Out of the darkness to the light—
The voice of Love in human form
    Hath foiled the legions of the night!

O happy they, whose faith and love
    Through grave and gate of death endure!
Thrice happy they, who from its sleep
    Rise to the vision of the pure!

"He giveth His Beloved Sleep."

HE giveth His beloved sleep—why then
    Should we the loved and lost so vainly
  weep!
We render but His own ; He takes again
    What only He in blessed peace can keep!

He giveth sleep—He, Who is named Love,
    He, Who for us Himself in flesh did weep ;
He curtaineth earth's couch around, above,
    And on it giveth His beloved sleep.

Soft is the spot where He, our Lord, hath lain,
    Amid the flowers His Holy Hands caressed ;
So may we sleep in Him, Who bore our pain,
    And to His own Beloved giveth rest !

He giveth sleep, He, Who slumbereth not ;
    Who keepeth Israel by day, by night !
He giveth sleep unto His own—and they,
    At last, shall wake in Him—the fadeless
      Light !

THE CHURCH.

"Jerusalem—the Mother of us all!"

"They shall prosper that love Thee!"

O MOTHER dear, what healing love
   Shall we Thy children, few and weak,
Bear to Thee from the Heaven above,
   Which Thou hast taught us how to seek!

We are but poor, yet rich in Thee;
   The heritage that Thou dost give
Is honour, love and liberty—
   For these alone we ask to live!

We cling to Thee through every ill;
   We follow Thee through storm and shine;
Our hearts shall teach Thy way and will,
   O Holy Mother, Church Divine!

Thou art the Spouse of Jesu's heart;
   Thou art the Home of Jesu's grace;
We love Thee for the love Thou art—
   Blest Image of the Saviour's Face!

O Mother dear, for Jesu's sake,
   Who is Thy Love, Who is Thy Life,
Into Thine arms Thy children take
   And shield them from a world of strife!

Bear them to Jesu's holy Feet,
   Keep them by Jesu's holy Side;
Be Thine, at last, to make them meet
   To reign with Him, the Crucified!

The Saviour and the Ship.

"And He was in the hinder part of the ship."
(St. Mat. iv. v. 38.)

THY Bark shall bear us on, O Lord!
    Thy children, ever safe within,
No terror of the night shall harm—
    Nor life, nor death, nor storm of sin!

For Thou art with us in the Ship;
    Thy Voice shall still the wintry sea—
And thus our hearts shall reach in peace
    The Haven where Thine own would be!

EUCHARISTIC.

"Lord, evermore give us this Bread!"

O KING of souls and Bread of men,
  Deliverer strong and Saviour, when
Hope's last, faint, quivering ray had gone—
Feed Thou our hearts again!

Lord, evermore give us this Bread!
O Thou, Who hast Thy children led
O'er worn and wasted, hungering ways,
Feed Thou as Thou hast fed!

Who would eat husks, when better far
Than holy Angels' dainties are—
Is freely offered—naught but sin
The sinner to debar!

O who would stand and linger still,
'Mid joys that fade and never fill,
When all that God can give awaits
The doer of His will!

Come, weary hearts, earth hath no woe,
No hunger and no need below,
God's Altar may not heal; "Eat!" "Drink!"
And in God's comfort go!

Eucharistic Prayer.

LORD, keep these wandering feet
   Within Thy path,
This erring heart and hand
   From works of wrath;
Thy way alone is peace,
From other ways release!

  O Body broken once,
     And Blood once shed,
  Heal now the broken heart,
     The bowéd head,
  The sorely-weeping eyes—
  Thou wilt not such despise!

  For Thou hast loved and wept,
     When once bereft;
  Upon the Cross Thy Wounds
     For such were cleft—
  O in Thy Riven Side
  Our sin and sorrow hide!

ADVENT.

Come, Master, Come!

COME, Master, come!
    I'm waiting in the gloom;
I'm groping in the night;
O Thou to Whom alike
Are darkness and the light,
Jesus, my Master, come!

Come, Master, come!
The way is long and hard—
The way which Thou hast trod;
Lead me by Thine own hand,
Almighty Son of God!
Come, gracious Master, come!

Come, Master, come!
Thy weary followers wait
In fasting, tears and prayer,
One awful, ceaseless fight,
One burden of sad care—
Come, Holy Master, come!

Come, Master, come!
Incarnate Mercy, come!
O by Thine own Self given

In love of life and death,
Be Thou our way to Heaven—
Come, blessed Master, come!

Come, Master, come!
In risen glory come—
Come in the clouds of light;
Come with Thy Heavenly host;
Dispel, dispel our night—
Triumphant Master, come!

Come, Master, come!
Come to Thy human home;
Redeem this land of Thine;
Make earth's remotest soil
Thine own dear Palestine—
Come, kingly Master, come!

Come, Master, come!
Thou wilt not surely stay;
The hour unknown is nigh—
We read it in Thy world;
'Tis written in the sky—
Come, faithful Master, come!

Come, Master, come!
It is Thy Word we plead;
The Spirit and the Bride,
And all that hear, say come!
Come with us to abide—
Jesus, my Master, come!

An Advent Thought.

"Lest coming suddenly He find you sleeping."
(*St. Mark* 13 : *v.* 36.)

Asleep, asleep—O life of pride,
For which a lowly Saviour died !
O love of Him—the Crucified !
To sleep when sin and death deride,
And awful wrath and judgment call,
And darkness hangeth over all !

Asleep—when Jesus bids thee wake,
While yet is time thy cross to take,
And light is springing o'er the hill—
Revealing Light of Heaven's will—
The Advent Light that is to come,
To lead thee, wanderer, to thy Home !

Awake, arise, thine armour don,
While yet is time to put it on—
To fight, to labour, while 'tis day,
To watch, to weep, to fast, to pray,
To struggle on in ceaseless strife
Unto the Throne of Light and Life !

But, Christian, heed ! thou mayst not go
Alone—unto that Throne aglow
With Love Divine—a Saviour's love,
Incarnate from the Heaven above !
Before that Throne thou mayst not stand,
But with thy brother hand in hand !

That crystal-mansioned Home of Grace
Can but reflect a brother's face !
Those golden gates may open wide
But for a brother by thy side !
Those pearly streets in Glory trod
By those whom Love hath brought to God !

"Waiting!"

Waiting—only waiting—till our God shall come;
Waiting—only waiting—till He lead us home;
Waiting—ever waiting—this our life and lot;
Waiting—ever waiting—still He cometh not!

Waiting—always waiting—waiting for our God,
Waiting 'neath His smile, and waiting 'neath His rod,
Seeing Him in gladness, feeling Him in peace,
Waiting till He bringeth sorrow's last release.

Waiting for a Saviour, Who shall make us glad,
Who shall give earth's needy all that Heaven had;
Who shall make all light where all hath been but gloom,
And on sin's sad desert make the roses bloom.

Waiting for a Kingdom, who have now a King,
Joy and peace and blessing It shall surely bring;
Banish every shadow, health to every sore—
Kingdom of Christ Jesus coming evermore!

Waiting for His glory, coming to our sight,
Coming, no man knoweth, hour of day or night;
O the perfect beauty of that Home above,
Which hath been erected for the hearts that love !

Waiting by a Manger, watching for a Star,
Of a Saviour's coming, seen by faith afar ;
Waiting now to welcome, waiting to adore
Him Whom angels worship, Him Who came before !

Waiting, Holy Master, give us grace to wait ;
Make us ever ready—never, never late !
Waiting, "up and doing," ready to go out,
When through Heaven's welkin rings the herald shout !

Waiting for a Coming, which shall be our joy—
Blessing to the Blessed, peace without alloy :
Advent shadows lessen—Christmas peal abroad
Glory Hallelujah to the coming Lord !

CHRISTMAS.

Hail, Holy Night!

HAIL, Holy Night!
    Night ever sweet
And ever bright!
    Hail, Holy Morn—
Hail hearts that greet
    A Saviour born!

Hail, Blessed Night,
    Night ever filled
With Heaven's light!
    Hail Angel Choirs,
Forever thrilled
    With pure desires!

Hail, gracious Night,
    So full of peace
And truth and right—
    Good will to men
Shall never cease
    Her voice again!

Hail, Night of Love—
  Most blest of nights,
Below, above!
  That maketh one
God's Heaven and earth,
  In Christ His Son!

Hail, Glorious Night
  Of Jesus' Birth—
The Saints' delight:
  O Christ our King,
Let all the earth
  Thy praises ring!

O Gates of Glory far Above!

O GATES of Glory far above,
That open at the voice of **Love**,
This Day of days,
To Songs of Praise—
Through you to earth
Your King has come
In human birth!

O shining hosts of sweetest song,
Who to His Monarch's train belong,
Waking the Night
To strains of Light,
And telling men
Their God hath come
To save again!

How shall our voices weak respond!
What offering fit and fair and fond
For this poor heart,
In its best art,
To take this day
To Bethlehem
So far away!

What shall we bring? our wreaths of flowers,
Our garlands green! our manhood's powers—
Our *myrrh* be this,

Thou King of Bliss,
Who once wast born
To rule Thine own
With Crown of thorn!

The *gold* of gentle woman's love,
So like to His, Who from above,
In Time did take,
And for our sake,
Our toil and fear,
A life of earth,
A mother dear.

And childhood's guilelessness and truth,
The *Frankincense* of blessed Youth
Our tribute be—
An Infancy
So pure and mild,
Like Thine alone,
O Holy Child!

Come, Gracious Jesu, come to all;
Be no poor heart beyond Thy call
This Blest of Days,
That wakes to praise—
O may it sing
Forevermore
Its Saviour King!

FEAST OF THE CIRCUMCISION.

"Thou shalt call His Name Jesus!"

O Name—sweet Name
Of Jesus, Child Divine,
Born once in Palestine!

O Name of Life!
All other names above,
Name of Incarnate Love!

Eternal Name,
Of all prevailing powers,
By Mercy now made ours!

The Name of God,
Of God on earth made man—
Who *would* be saved now can!

O Name of grace!
Our only Name to plead
In each and every need!

Jesus, My All!
All praise be ever Thine,
My Lord, my Love Divine!

LENT.

We need to Fast.

"This kind goeth not out but by prayer and fasting."
(*St. Mat.* 17: v. 21.)

We need to fast!
Our life is full
Of sense and sin;
We need control
And self-command,
That grace and truth
May enter in.

We need to weep—
So sore our wounds
Of daily fight;
We need to bow
In sorest shame,
If we would know
The healing Light.

We need to pray—
O nothing more!
Each tempted hour,
To kneel alone,
In lull of strife,
And from His Hand
To gain new power.

We need to weep
And fast and pray,
Like Him of old—
Our Lord and God,
Who thus shall bring
At last His own
Into His Fold!

"Watch and Pray!"

O WATCH and pray! we never know
  The hour that flesh may yield;
The soldier of the Captain Christ
  Sleeps never on the field.

O watch and pray, thou troubled one,
  In thy Redeemer's might!
O never give the battle up,
  O watch and pray and fight!

O watch and pray, thou tempted one,
  In thy dear Master's power,
What loving heart would hear again,
  "Could ye not watch one hour?"

O watch and pray and struggle on,
  Strength cometh with the strife,
He giveth Love to love that bleeds,
  He giveth Life for life!

A Lenten Thought in Rhyme.

O LITTLE life of ours—
    So few, so poor the years !
A way of sadness and of shame,
    A path of sighs and tears !

Man riseth to his work,
    And goeth forth to fight ;
The noonday brings but weariness,
    And after that the night !

The harvest is of sin ;
    The gleaning but of tares ;
We rest at weary eventide,
    'Mid cold and cumbering cares.

We fall from smiles to tears ;
    We leap from tears to smile :
Our happiness is to forget
    A little, lingering while !

And yet this is not wise ;
    This is not as we read
In that dear Life, Divine and blest,
    Which is our Christian Creed !

That Heart, Which stooped from Heaven,
    Because It felt our woe,
And lived and loved and died and rose
    For fallen hearts below.

Methinks I read therein
    Another tale and truth,
How in the grace of Christ our Lord
    Is found eternal youth !

The everlasting health
    Which comes from God alone,
The grace, the mercy, and the peace,
    Which reign about His Throne !

From Him, Who went about,
    Beloved of earth and Heaven,
His Life a way for each and all,
    In endless pity given !

He walked with wayworn men ;
    He sat beside their feast ;
The Friend of sinners and of saints,
    The highest and the least !

He healed their sick and sad ;
    He even raised their dead ;
The Blessed Son of God, Who "had
    Nowhere to lay His Head" !

He wept with those who wept,
   The many all around—
The tears of Jesus fell and made
   Our hearts a holy ground!

" Tell me no more that life
   Is but an empty dream ;
Tell me no longer things that are,
   Are only what they seem ! "

There is a better life ;
   There is a brighter love ;
There is a way from earth and sin
   To Life and Light above!

Labour is blest in Christ,
   And victory hath a Crown !
The soul that hopes and waits in **God**,
   Is nevermore cast down !

This life may be a *Lent*
   To weary hearts and worn ;
But Lent of fast and tear and **prayer**
   Leadeth to Easter morn !

PALM SUNDAY.

The Palm beside the Cross.

THE Palm beside the Cross,
   The Crown of Life above,
Earth's weary looking up
   Unto the Heavens of love!

And Angel voices sweet
   Telling our hearts to-day,
What once their Leader told
   A Virgin far away—

That She her Lord should bear,
   The message which he gave,
And Jesus is the Name
   With which He came to save!

O happy hearts to-day—
   To hear the Angels' voice,
To hail a Saviour's Love
   And with the palms rejoice!

O weeping hearts of earth,
   And waving Palms no more—
To stand beneath the Cross,
   The cruel Cross He bore!

O holy hearts and pure,
  On whom the blood-drops fall,
That cleanse from sin and shame,
  A Cross of Life for all !

Lord, bring us by Thy Cross—
  Thy way of Passion's Palm,
Through tears and toil and strife,
  To Resurrection's calm !

The Glory of that Morn
  When palms shall yield to flowers,
And all things everywhere
  In Jesus Christ are ours !

GOOD FRIDAY.

"Lord, have mercy upon us!"

THOU, Who hast known our mortal need,
   In each and every pang,
When every human sin and woe
Upon Thy Cross did hang—

O by Thy want upon the Tree,
Thy wounds and throat of fire—
Bring, Shepherd Good, Thy thirsting sheep
To streams of sweet desire!

O by Thy Cross for sinners borne,
And by the grave for sinners rent,
And by Thy tears for sinners shed,
And by Thy Head for sinners bent!

O by Thy glory now and grace,
And by Thy Throne at God's right hand,
And by Thy Crown of Light and Life,
Bring us into Thy Promised Land!

"Father, forgive them!"

"Father, forgive them, for they know not what they do!"

FATHER, forgive them—each and all,
   They surely know not what they do;
My death is none the less for them,
   And all confirms Thy Word as true!

'Twas pardoning Love alone that led
   My Heart from Heaven to bleed and die,
Upon a Cross of human shame,
   Beneath Judea's darkened sky.

'Twas Love that bore the taunts of hate,
   The ignominy and the scorn,
The mockery of purple robe,
   The cruel, cruel crown of thorn!

O by that Love, which is Thy Name,
   Father of all, for love of Me,
Forgive them what they now have done,
   They know not that it is to Thee!

EASTER.

"He is Risen!"

THE night of grief hath passed away;
   The morning Light of God appears:
Be still, O weary heart, and rest;
   Be scattered, O ye groping fears!

The Rays of my Redeemer's Brow
   Shall rend the mists of doubt and sin—
There is no shadow in that Land
   Where His Beloved have entered in!

He is the Lamb; He is the Light;
   His Hand all tears shall wipe away;
And they shall know, who now believe,
   He is the Life, the Truth, the Way!

The questions that we ask so oft,
   As on earth's path we pause in pain,
Shall need no other word than His,
   Who lived and died and rose again!

"Lift up your Heads!"

LIFT up your heads, ye Gates of gold!
   Ye doors of Glory open wide!
Behold, He comes—the King of kings;
   He comes, Who was the Crucified!

His Crown prepare, of priceless gems,
   For such a Brow earth hath none meet!
On such a day she can but strew
   Her flowers of praise beneath His feet!

O LOVED and lost so long ago—
   Risen from our sight, beyond the dead,
What can our faltering footsteps do
   But follow where Thine own have led!

O'er hill and vale, o'er land and sea,
   Wherever trod those Feet Divine,
That made all hearts forever glad,
   And every land a Palestine!

We follow where Thy Love hath led,
   Fed by Thy Hand, Thy Body given;
And guided by Thy Grace shall come
   From Cross to Crown, from earth to Heaven!

"The Resurrection and the Life!"

O RISEN with healing in Thy wings!
Thou Lord of lords and King of kings;
Thou Conqueror of death and grave,
Be Thine the joy Thy triumph gave!

O death, where is thine aching sting!
O grave, what trophies shalt thou bring!
O Life, O Love, O Bliss Divine!
O Heaven of Heavens forever mine!

They live who die; they wake who sleep;
They laugh who mourn; they sing who weep;
They rise and chant His endless praise,
Who won them from earth's weary ways!

His wounds a Fount, the thorns a Crown!
All glory for the life laid down;
All toils and tears forever past;
A Rest that shall forever last!

O Risen King! O Holy Lord!
We do believe Thy Blessed Word;
We look to Thee through earth's dark strife—
The Resurrection and the Life!

WHIT-SUNDAY.

O Loving Spirit of Our God!

"Let Thy Loving Spirit lead me forth into the Land of Righteousness!" (Ps. 143: v. 10.)

O LOVING Spirit of our God,
    Thou Mover of the mortal heart,
Enter Thy shrine this Holy Day
    And life and love and joy impart!

Breathe on this dust of time and sin;
    Breathe on these clods of earth below,
Thou Burning Breath of God descend
    And warm them into Heaven's glow!

Breathe on these bones of dry despair,
    Within this shadowy vale of tears;
O come and clothe with living flesh!
    Dispel the wasting, waging fears!

Breathe on the hearts that know Thee not,
    That never knew God's blessed love,
And lead them forth from sin and self
    Unto the better Life above—

The Land of Righteousness and Rest,
    Where reigneth Christ, the King of kings,
O Spirit Blest, breathe on our hearts,
    Who art the Healing of His Wings!

THE HOLY MARTYRS.

The Holy Innocents.

THEY fought no battles, yet they won their Crown;
They knew it not, yet was their life laid down—
For Jesus did they live and did they die ;
Their Innocence became their meed on high!

Thy Martyrs, Lord, in every age are those—
Earth's flowers transplanted ere their petals close ;
And buds of hope, which, since she cannot prize,
Ope only in Thy vernal Paradise !

Thine Innocents, who trod the living way,
Stained with Thy blood and theirs in earth's dark day,
The seed of sweetness and the germ of power,
The Church's blessing and her Bridal dower !

Lord, may we learn to live like them: do **Thou**
With holy innocence our hearts endow,
To love Thee only, ever, first and last;
So shall this tyranny be overpast !

The Army of the Lord.

THEY lifted up their hearts to God,
   And found Him in each living clod
Of earth around, whereon of old
The story of His Love was told !

What recked they then the rack, the stake,
Endured for their Redeemer's sake :
O what to them the fangs, the fire—
It could not touch their heart's desire !

They were the Army of the Lord,
Wielding aloft His Spirit's Sword ;
And how they fought, for what they fell
Let earth's Te Deums endless tell !

O make us worthy, Lord, like them,
To hold Thy Battle-Banner's hem,
Faithful in life, in death to Thee—
The Truth that makes Thy children free !

THE CHURCH'S MINISTRY

"The Noble Army of Martyrs."

Dedicated to the Sainted Memory of the Priestly Brothers and the Sisters, fallen at Memphis, Tennessee: A.D., 1878.

THE hero's sword has carved its way
    Through seas of blood to crowns of gold;
They gloried in the battle shock,
    The doughty paladins of old!

No fear nor fainting in the strife;
    They fought—they conquered or they fell;
The gleaming pages of the past
    Delight their chivalry to tell!

And yet 'twere easy task to wage
    A warfare with the cruel wrong;
The heart of manhood leaps to arms,
    And, striking, sings its battle-song!

Give them all meed of honest praise,
   The man, the hero, and the king;
To strong-armed Right upon its throne,
   Let earth her proudest pæans sing!

But hark! beneath I hear a voice,
   So sweet and soothing and serene,
Like melody of angel harps—
   It is the Martyrs' song, I ween:

The song of those who took their lives
   Within their gentle, lowly hands,
To do the work of Christ their Lord
   In life and death, on seas and lands.

They loved no less the glowing light
   That fell on fields and flowers and home;
That followed them in tempting gleam,
   Where'er they rest, where'er they roam.

They love no less the earth below,
   So beautiful with God's own love;
But O their vision is beyond,
   Unto the Paradise above!

God's Saints and Martyrs—who are they?
   His holy heroes—can it be
That such still live in file and rank
   In only earth's obscurity?

Unarmed, unaided and unknown,
   Obedient to the Voice above,
The lonely warriors of the Cross—
   God's Chivalry of faith and love!

No trump is heard to summon them;
   No bannered might to urge them on;
In silent watches of the heart
   Their battles oftenest are won!

By fever-beds of pain and woe,
   Where manhood shrinks and courage fails,
And life is stripped unto its core,
   And human pride no more avails;

When all is dark and all is drear,
   And earth's poor comforts all have fled,
His ministers of Grace appear
   To soothe and cheer the dying head.

These are Thy messengers, O Lord,
   Incarnate Christ, Thine own are they,
Who find Thy little ones in need,
   Who help and heal, who watch and pray!

O blest, thrice blest, be ever they
   Who lose themselves in such a love,
And find each day a holy step
   Unto the better life above!

Whose home is only where God calls,
    Whose post is where His love appoints;
Whose sacrifice of heart is seen
    Upon the brow His grace anoints.

These are God's children, tried and true,
    His Martyr-army noble, blest;
They that have borne His Cross and laid
    Themselves upon it unto rest!

The Priests of the Most High God.

To Christopher Billopp Wyatt, of beloved memory!

THEY are, O Lord, Thine own,
  Sealed by Thy Heavenly Hand,
And sent throughout the land—
To win unto Thy pitying Throne
The lost, yet loving, and the lone!

Commissioned by Thy Might,
 O Prophet, King and Priest,
 The lowly and the least
Of earth, like Thee—yet in Thy sight
The warriors of the Crowned Right!

Bearing Thy vessels, Lord,
 Cleanly through sloughs of sin,
 Aloft 'mid earthly din,
That to Thy children ever give
The Bread by which the dying live!

Troubled, yet not cast down,
 Because upheld by Thee,
 'The Lifted on the Tree!'
Whose every pang from hatred's frown
Won for His own a thornless Crown!

These be the souls that bring
   Peace everywhere they go;
   Their lives serenely flow:
They make earth's weary wastes to sing;
They are true courtiers of their King.

For these Thy Name we bless,
   Thy Treasure, Lord, and ours;
   And with Thy given powers,
In Thy dear steps and theirs we press
To reach Thy Heavens of Righteousness!

O Brother, Father, Friend—
   True, trusted, tempered, tried,
   Whose faith no act belied—
May He, Who doth such only lend,
Unto our need such others send!

THE CHURCH'S WORK.

"Give!"

GIVE!—what to give? a word? wherefore?
A thought? ah now! a deed?
Yes all and evermore!

To give is Godlike, for God gave—
To be like Him in love,
Who came from Heaven to save!

What shall I give? Myself!—like God,
Who laid His glory down,
And on it for us trod!

O little life for endless love!
O barren, fruitless tree!
What place for thee above?

God help us still—O Thou, Whose Grace
Can lift the lowest soul,
Find for my feet a place!

And when at last, O Lord, I stand
Before Thy Glory's Throne,
Fill Thou my empty hand!

"Where hast thou gleaned to-day?"

WHERE hast thou gleaned to-day?
Say, toiling heart,
Weary and worn with grief,
Show me thy scanty sheaf!
O hast thou found the way!
Where hast thou gleaned to-day?

Where hast thou gleaned to-day,
Poor, pilgrim child?
Amid the blessed grain,
For hunger's aching pain;
Or 'mid the dark decay—
Where hast thou gleaned to-day?

Where hast thou gleaned to-day,
Frail, fainting heart?
Among the pure and blest,
Towards the dim land of Rest?
Dear Heart, tell me not, nay!
Where hast thou gleaned to-day?

Where hast thou gleaned to-day,
Tempted and tried?
'Mid siren hosts of sin,

Striving thy soul to win?
Gleaner, darest thou say,
Where thou hast gleaned to-day?

Where hast thou gleaned to-day,
Faithful and strong?
Behold true love is mute!
Thy hands are full of fruit,
Before God's throne to lay,
Beyond this gleaning day!

Love's Labour.

THY God hath spoken, "Follow Me!"
   Thy labour must be full and free—
  A holy Art!
My Kingdom is the Home of Love,
Which streameth from the Heavens above,
   To every heart!

All life is labour, and thy choice
Must be, with all-consenting voice,
   To have it so:
Its glory is to work with God—
To find Him in each lowly clod
   Of earth below!

He walketh still with living men,
Within the garden fair again,
   Of Truth and Grace;
And thou—His child—whate'er thy state,
Content "to labour and to wait,"
   Shalt see His Face!

Live that thou have no fear to die,
With thought of judgment ever nigh
   And heart of love;
So shall thy pathway here below
With light and blessing sweetly glow,
   Like Heaven above!

"Why stand ye here all the day idle?"

WORK, work, while the Master calleth,
    Work on 'while 'tis called to-day;'
Work, work, while the Light remaineth,
    And shineth on the way!

Work, work, for the holy Kingdom,
    Work on for the Crown of rest,
That is promised to the faithful,
    The righteous and the blest!

For all the world is a vineyard,
    But a vineyard of the Lord,
And He calleth us to labour
    By His own Holy Word.

There are stones and thorns around us;
    There is foul offence within,
And to him who idly standeth
    The wages are of sin!

Work on and look ever upward,
    Falter not beneath the Cross—
To fall by the weary wayside
    Would be eternal loss!

There is rest—at last in Jesus!
   There is peace about His Throne,
Who trod for us once the wine-press,
   Aweary and alone!

Who cometh again in Glory,
   In brightness above the sun—
Oh, joy to thy heart, my brother,
   He saith to thee, "Well done!"

"Labourers together with God."

OUR lives were lowly—lost indeed,
Had we no better voice to heed
    Than those around:
Our labour were but pain and grief,
An endless toil, without relief,
    On barren ground!

It were no life to live as they,
Who eat and drink, and sleep and play,
    And brutely die!
God breathed His life within man's heart,
And made his soul the shrine of art—
    His Own on high!

The Glories of His Holy Throne
Were never meant for them alone
    Who stand around:
Their radiance pierceth throught the night
To thee, who labouring on aright,
    His way hast found!

Lift up thy heart; look unto God,
And find Him in each fragrant sod
    Of earth below;
For where once trod those Blessed Feet
Should be a labour ever sweet,
    As Thou shalt know!

No Time to Lose!

WITH all a world to save, He went away,
    Into a desert place apart to pray—
The night in prayer, so not to lose the day,
O what shall idling men henceforward say!

He prayed, Who had Himself no need to pray,
He walked by faith, Who was Himself the Way,
Using the night, Who was Himself the Day,
O why should men to go to God delay!

A Final Question?

O SOULS are dying all around,
    While we are half asleep;
We laugh and jest and trifle on,
    While half the world doth weep!

We talk of Christ, the Son of God,
    And what He came to give—
Were it not better less to *talk*,
    And more like Christ to *live!*

MISCELLANEOUS.

Shadows.

A LITTLE word—soon spoken,
    In petulance and pain ;
A golden link once broken,
    And never whole again !

Upon the brow a shadow,
    Upon the lip a play,
The wealth of El Dorado
    Can never buy away !

A shaft of sin and sorrow,
    From heart to heart of love—
And O, the sad to-morrow
    And the one Heaven above!

O why should the true-hearted
    Be to its own unkind,
Why should sweet love be parted
    And scattered to the wind!

O why to all so smiling
   Save to the one alone,
All other hearts beguiling,
   But that we call our own!

O mystery of loving!
   O wilful, tearful way!
That lingers in the shadow
   And trifles with the day!

"Thou Sendest Rain."

(Ps., 65, v. 11.)

THEY fairly laugh—the little flowers,
    They laugh beneath the rain;
They lift their petals toward the sky,
    And grateful laugh again!

The blushing rose, the graceful vine,
    The lilies fair and sweet;
The tender grass, the wild flower gay,
    Alike do laugh and greet.

They quiver to their gentle souls,
    In happy, gracious glee,
And every leaf and every drop
    A lesson is to me.

O blessed rain, that comes to all—
    The evil and the good,
That on the just and unjust too,
    Showers daily, needful food!

O blessed drops that eager fall,
    To do your holy task—
Like God's own love, that ever comes
    Before His children ask!

O gentle flowers that sweetly speak
   His word, His way, His will,
Who made of old His world in love,
   And loveth, blesseth still !

The Parish Church.

(St. P—— in the H——s.)

A HOLY spot, from hundred years of prayer;
Pity the heart that could not worship there!
A Temple from the eternal hills around,
Their quarried life on this all-hallowed ground:
Transepts and nave and apse, buttressed and towered,
Crowning a hill, 'mid glorious oaks embowered;
With many a restful grave upon the slope,
To tell the tale of lowly faith and hope!
The mingled song of bird and rustling trees,
Responding to the perfumed summer breeze—
Sweet Nature's psalm of ceaseless love and life,
Bidding us turn aside from daily strife,
To enter here and meditate and pray,
To rest awhile upon the weary way!

Science and Faith.

SCIENCE and Faith—are not both true and twin?
Both seek to know; both strive to enter in:
If one the higher looks—to the eternal spheres,
It is their music that the other hears!

Both struggle in a world of want and woe,
And both must watch each step where'er they go;
Yes, in a darksome world both feel their way,
And look beyond it to the perfect day!

And O, if one upon the knees must fall,
And lift its heart to Him Who ruleth all—
Shall not the other learn, with humble mind,
He can protect, Whom yet it cannot find!

Love guards them both, if only both would know,
Making one aim and end to all below:
Love is the only staff of strength, I ween,
On which the child and sage alike may lean!

We rise from Nature up to Nature's God ;
And Faith beholds Him in each living sod ;
He makes the rose to bloom, the grain to grow,
And human hearts with gratitude to glow !

One Power, one Force, one Law, one Life, one Love,
'Seen darkly now—awhile—then known above';
One Lord, one Faith, one Hope to mortals given,
To lead them on and satisfy in Heaven !

Charles Kingsley.

DIED JANUARY 24TH, 1875.

WEEP for the noble dead,
　　At rest on England's soil—
His home and proudly ours!
His earthly labour done,
So soon the battle won!
The manhood of his powers
Beneath the silent sod:
Weep for the noble dead,
Gone to his rest, with God!

Methinks 'twere better so—
The soldier in his rank,
The hero on the field,
The face before the foe;
Better to fall in fight,
Expire upon a shield,
Than still the war to wage,
And then to droop and die
In sad defeat of age!

The vineyard of the Lord
Is strewn with fallen fruit,
And why we cannot tell!
We only hear God say,
Ye hungering souls of earth,
Eat and ye shall do well;
My servants' lives I give—
Eat of this fallen fruit
And ye shall surely live!

No better food of Heaven
Than lives like this we weep,
Single, serene and pure,
A spirit born to power,
A mind of gift and grace,
A life born to endure,
A manly life and strong,
The faithful friend to right
And fearless foe to wrong!

Kingsley, thy name shall live
When kingly names have died,
And men shall love to read
And never cease to glow
Beneath thy genius' spell,
The vigour of thy creed—
"Hypatia," "Alton Locke,"
And "Amyas," heart of oak
And arm of living rock!

All these shall tell us still
How men may live and love,
And seek a better life ;
How never crown was won
Without a cross, and peace
Ne'er conquered but through strife !
How only " grace and truth "
Are armor of the Lord
For fresh and valiant youth !

All honour then to him,
" The loyal heart and true,"
Who speaketh while we weep !
All glory to our God,
Who taketh what He gave,
And giveth holy sleep—
For thee a happy rest,
Thy memory in our hearts
Benign, beloved, blest !

"Only Another Reverse!"

(Candahar—July, 1880.)

ONLY another reverse—
　　Nothing, O nothing worse!
Two thousand men or more
Wiped from the face of earth:
O, it is only war!

Some men of the rank and file,
Many a thousand mile
Away, o'er land and mount
And sea and sand and sun—
Naught of any account!

Never to come home again!
Hundreds of Englishmen
Leaving mother and wife
To weep and wail alone;
O, that is only life!

And why did they go to fight?
Was it for wrong or right,
For some great, noble end,
God's truth to vindicate?
Who did those soldiers send?

"Never mind!"   "Reasons of state!"
And now it is too late;
They are dead—let them go!
But let some one beware—
Above things are not so!

Will you men of power not learn
That e'en a worm will turn!
And the Lord on His Throne
Only waits for a while
To avenge every moan!

"Only another reverse"—
Another added curse
To the sin of the race,
That darkens weary earth
And hides from it God's face!

President Garfield.

BRAVE, patient soul, we never knew
   How great thou wert ; nor yet our love
How deeply loyal, till it flew--
   A Nation's arm to bear thee up,
A Nation's tears to overflow
   The brimming cup !

We all were struck to earth with thee ;
   Yet with thy faith we rise again,
Firm with the fibre of the free,
   That cannot fail, that cannot die,
Because it looks beyond the storm
   To God on high !

The lesson thou hast taught shall live ;
   Men pass away, and but their deeds
Survive on earth ; and thine shall give
   To generations yet unborn,
Strength to achieve, and grace to wear
   Earth's crown—of thorn !

On a Birthday.

LIKE touches of an angel harp,
  Soothing the memories of care,
This day of thine brings to the soul
But notes of joy and love and prayer!

Where are they—O the winged years,
Where are they flown, so sweetly given!
Ask of our hearts, O Love Divine,
And be their answer—unto Heaven!

Love hath no aching age, and time
Is but a name, a breath, a sigh—
We live within the hearts we love,
And all but love itself shall die!

O sacred memories of the past,
That thronging seek to guide my pen—
Ye must be voiceless still and wait,
Like all things that shall live again!

But one dear thought shall be my theme,
My birthday gift from Heaven above,
A prayer of blessing unto Him,
Who knew on earth a Mother's love!

Farewell!

"GONE TO SEA," JULY—, 1877.

O LOYAL heart and liberal hand,
To all that need a magic wand
Of kindly power,
And wealth—the stewardship of God
To all upon His living sod,
Not blest as thou—
God's mercies follow thee
And thine beyond the sea!

The waves shall whisper of a Love—
E'en God's Infinity above,
In which alone
The motive of thy life is found;
A vessel to God's haven bound,
So staunch and strong,
And full of food for men,
Who ask and ask again!

The mirrored heavens shall sweetly tell
By day, by night, to ocean's swell,
Of Him, Whose seat
Of glory fills the rolling spheres,
Whose Name is Life to human ears
And weary hearts;
To all that sigh release—
Light, rest, eternal peace!

Love's blessings speed thy winged bark ;
At eventide and morning hark
To distant prayers !—
A tide of love to push thy prow
Over old Ocean's favoring brow ;
Until at last
The havened joy to see,
Where thou and thine would be !

The Wreck of "The Atlantic."

APRIL 1st, 1873.

SILENCE throughout the land! Silence and prayer
To Him, Whose judgments fill all hearts with fear—
A prayer for those who by death's ruthless hand
Were hurled into the night, into the depths,
Unto the unknown land!

It was a night of ocean calm and peace;
A thousand souls lay down to cradled dreams—
Of home before and home behind—sweet rest!
Dreams of this fitful life, and dreams perchance
Already of the blest!

O God! what is that shock, that awful cry!
What means this giant struggle with the night!
"O what!" "How!" "Where!" A thousand shrieks proclaim
The agony of hope—and then despair,
Of death without a name!

O God! and is this life, and is this death?
To die upon the very rocks that guard
The land we love—where love awaits in prayer!
Is this a welcome home, a welcome meet
For those who seek one there!

And yet Love rules the world—'twas blessed Love
That ruled the wind and sea that wintry night!
Love spread her wings to shelter and to save,
The deathless love of Him—the Christ Divine,
Who trod Gennesaret's wave!

Love ruled the gallant souls—alas too few!
Who night and death defied, and freely gave
The worthy holocaust of life and strength;
Who bore on their staunch hearts the worn
Till succour came at length!   [and weak,

Love sent the fisher-boats, faithful to Him
Who called the fishermen of Galilee:
Love ruled their sturdy hearts to dare and die,
The love of Him Who for His own hath homes
Beyond the darkest sky!

Love ruled the hero heart, His Master's liege,
His Master's servant on that sullen coast:
Love gave him skill and power to fight the wave,
To wrest from horrid death a priceless life—
All honour to God's brave!

O Life, O Love that could survive the storm;
That could endure when all was dark and dread!
O faith and hope that trod serene the deck,
And gently bore the loved on angel wings
Above the deathly wreck!

O love of wedded hearts, in death as true
As in meridian hour of life and joy!
O love that sank in last and locked embrace—
It is not death to die in such a bond,
In such a living grace!

O blessed hearts that live the better life,
And only find in death your regal crown!
O holy faith that sees its Lord Divine
As near on Nova Scotia's fatal coast
As erst in Palestine!—

God greet ye all! The wild waves be your rest!
Sing sweetly, ocean winds, your requiem!
Bear softly, ocean depths, your holy dead!
Weep o'er your conquered foes, and as ye weep
Bend low the crested head!

O Ocean—to our hearts a name of doom!
O seas that roll between our hearts' desires!
O billows that too terribly portray
Uncertain life! thank God—if ye have taught
Some erring hearts to pray!

O lonely hearts that mourn in stricken homes,
In every land beneath a Christian sun,
Be comforted—it is your Father's will!
His word, Who to your hearts as to the storm,
Doth whisper, "peace, be still!"

Ye have not long to wait! The night of woe
Is but a night! Already do we see
The flush of Heaven's morn!—'Faint not, but
 pray!'
So shall ye meet your loved soon in the land
Where reigns eternal day!

Silence and tears throughout the startled land!
Prayers to the God, 'Whose footsteps are not
 known;
Whose path is in the waters of the deep;'
Who leads His children home by many ways,
And gives them blessed sleep!

In Camp,

near the Fountain of Elisha and the site of ancient Jericho, March 30, 1871.

AND can this be the very land,
Blessed by Jehovah's guiding hand!
And do I tread the very sod
Pressed once by my Incarnate God!

And is this too the very breeze—
This whispering music of the trees—
This balmy air I'm breathing now
Once fanned my dear Redeemer's brow!

And can that be the very peak
Whereon once stood the Prophet meek,
And gazed o'er Jordan's valley wide,
Before he laid him down and died!

Those mountains, bathed in orient light,
Were they once trod by Israel's might!
And gleamed the sword in this bright sun,
Waved by the warrior son of Nun!

And did these very mountains round,
Once echo Israel's battle sound!
This spot—a haughty city's wall,
Crumbling before that clarion call!

This sacred river, gliding by,
Was it for Israel's sake once dry;
Thrice smitten by the man of God,
That His elect might pass dry-shod!

And did these very heavens once ope
To realize a prophet's hope!
The sound that on my senses steals,
The roll of Heaven's chariot wheels!

And still more holy thought and dear—
Did once my Saviour sojourn here!
Who, washed in Jordan's quiet tide,
His followers hearts hath sanctified!

And on yon mountain, lone and bare,
Laden with sorrow, toil and care,
Did He, in tempter's subtlest hour,
Show unto earth and Heaven His power!

O sacred air! O blessed light!
O vision pure! O fancy bright!
O fainting heart, thou must not fail
To drink the bliss of Jordan's vale!

Refreshed and hallowed by this hour,
Seek in its dreams the Spirit's power;
And, blessed by all its visions rare,
Breathe thou again thy childhood's prayer:

Father, I pray, my footsteps lead;
For I am full of sin and need—
Weary and worn I seek but Thee;
Father, in mercy, look on me!

A pilgrim, and yet not as some,
Who pardon hope *because* they come,
I follow Him along the way,
Who led us unto Thee to pray.

I come, I kneel, I seek the wave,
Where He hath washed, Who died to save:
As Jordan's water cools my brow,
O Thou who healest, heal me now!

Protect me, guide me evermore;
Make my path straight from Jordan's shore:
As Thou Thy Son in love hast given,
O may that Love lead me to Heaven!

"Domine, Quo Vadis?"

A LEGEND OF THE VIA APPIA.

IT was the quiet eventide,
    Dusk veiled the earth and sky,
As swiftly through Rome's closing gates
A dark clad form swept by.

An aged man of stature grand,
His beard of snowy white,
And his eagle eye distended
With fear and shame and flight!

"O whither now so fast, my Friend?"
The mailed sentry cries;
A muttered word like "Appia,"
The muffled voice replies.

The soldier turns upon his heel,
The old man hastens on—
What recks the Roman or his Rome,
Their noblest teacher gone!

"Why, father, on the Way so late?"
The plodding peasant asks.
He rushes by with eager feet,
And murmurs "distant tasks."

And thus saluting, pass him by
The travellers few and stray,
Who tread with hastening homeward steps
Rome's proudest Appian way.

And now his coward heart grows light,
More firmly falls his tread;
Yet still, as by the weight of shame,
He bows his hoary head.

But lo, what form approaches him!
Who can this stranger be,
Who late and lone and wearily
Crosses the Roman lea?

The old man starts with look of dread;
His fears resume their sway,
As nearer draws the wanderer
Upon the Appian way.

They meet, they gaze—O wondrous sight!
O cry of awe and shame!
The old man falls upon his knees,
And breathes a Holy Name!

But yet the stranger halteth not—
One glance of His sad eye,
And still upon the Appian
Towards Rome He passeth by.

"*O Domine, quo vadis?*" cries
In terror, doubt and pain,
The aged fugitive from Rome,
And crieth yet again.

The Master turns and pauseth now,
O calm and sweet reply:
"Another cross for Me is raised,
I go to Rome to die!"

"I go, for suffering and death
Must come to Me or thee;
I gladly go to die again
For those who fail and flee!"

"O Lord, forgive Thy faithless one!"
The sinner's answering moan,
"Crush me not with Thy perfect love,
Return Thou to Thy Throne!"

Call me Thy Peter nevermore,
Unstable rock am I;
One last and only boon I crave,
That Thou wilt let me die!"

Our tale is told—St. Peter's name
Is sweet to Christian ear—
Gem in the martyr crown of gold,
The Church delights to wear.

O friend who lovest Christ in truth,
Seek thou the Appian way;
There is a little church hard by,
Where faint hearts love to pray.

Be not afraid to enter there,
Though it be holy ground;
A coward heart its Saviour lost,
Was by its Saviour found!

A Christmas Ballad,

From the German.

LIE still, my child, and sweetly sleep,
   While angels hover round thy cot;
In Heaven they see God's blessed face—
   They ever watch, they slumber not!

How soft thy couch!—Thy Saviour laid
   On wood and stone His infant head,
In manger dark, on straw and hay,
   While thou art blessed with cradle-bed.

Untroubled flows thy little life;
No power disturbs thy holy rest—
Thy Lord was born to storm and strife;
A thousand foes around Him pressed!

May God reveal forevermore
   Jesus—His gracious Son—in thee,
Thy soul to know and to adore
   What thou in *Christ, the Child*, may'st see!

Sleep, darling babe, sleep on in peace,
   And when God makes thee strong and wise,
May'st thou in spirit too increase
   And reach thy home beyond the skies!

A Centennial Hymn.

JULY 4TH, 1876.

O THOU, in Whom the nations live,
    And by Whose Word the people stand,
Who all things good dost ever give—
    The Light and Truth of every land!

With Whom one day of earth and time
    Are as a thousand years of grace,
And all an Empire's proudest prime
    Is but a day before Thy Face—

To Thee, the Source of Love and Law,
    An Empire, grand as ever known,
Would bow in gratitude and awe—
    Before the Glory of Thy Throne!

A hundred years of eager life,
    They come to bring as tribute meet—
The trophies of their toil and strife,
    To lay at their Redeemer's feet.

Through mists of error, clouds of sin,
    O'er wreck and ruin of their make,
They crowd Thy Temple doors within,
    And plead that Thou no vengeance take

Thou art the Nations' Lord and God,
  As true and tender unto them,
As erst upon Judea's sod
  To her who touched Thy garment's hem!

Forgive the wrongs that we have done,
  Our lust of eye and pride of life;
So little of the right race run,
  Our hearts and hands with passion rife.

O Thou, Whose glory is to save,
  Forgive the creatures of Thy hand,
To whom Thy loving kindness gave
  Our own, our dear, our native land!

Which led our Fathers o'er the sea,
  To shores of virgin life and love—
A continent so fair and free—
  To found a City from above:

A City where no foes offend,
  Where light and sweetness should abound,
And every life fulfil its end,
  And every spot be holy ground!

Forgive Thy children, Lord, we pray,
  That this is but a picture still;
And be our hundred years to-day
  A consecration to Thy will!

"The Crescent and the Cross."

WHENCE comes that moan across the sea—
That rending cry of agony,
Which thrills our souls and fills our eyes,
And maketh hearts of stone to rise?

It is a brother's wail of fear—
A brother's anguish loud and near,
A brother's blood, a sister's shame,
A Christian people's trampled fame!

And can it be that Christ has died,
With such a horror close beside!
Is this the world to which He came,
And gave in love His Holy Name!

Is this His Earth, is this His Race,
Is this the glory of His Face,
That eighteen centuries of light
Should wane before the Crescent's night!

O where the blood that coursed in glow
Through Europe's pulses while ago,
And rushed in chivalry of might
To recue Syria's holy site!

That grandly struck its mortal blow,
And freely poured its brightest flow,
To win and cleanse from Turkish horde
The Land, which gave us Christ the Lord!

O where the thrill of noblest faith
That triumphed even in its death,
And counted all things else but loss,
So it might fall beneath the Cross!

Where Godfrey's zeal and Tancred brave,
The best, the truest Europe gave—
The Paladins, who bore their part;
Where " Richard of the lion-heart " !

So needed now—O nevermore!
Heroic spirit gone before!
Return, renew, infuse, inspire
Our arms with strength, our hearts with fire!

Call this mistaken, if you will,
And name it folly at its fill;
And speak of soberness and sense,
The age of prudence, pounds and pence:

' The Christians are but so in name,
A mere illusion, empty fame,
In error oft, in practice poor,
A beggar crouching at the door.'

And we, the cautious and the cold,
We are the Pharisees of old,
Phylacteries as broad as then,
As anxious to be seen of men.

Our prayers and praise from cushioned pew;
Salvation for selected few!
What recks "Enlightment" to-day,
"A paltry Province far away!"

O age of caution, craft and cant,
Of reason, roguery and rant;
Of faith so fanciful and frail,
Of fancy faithless to avail!

O shall the Son of Man to come,
Find faith upon the earth His home,
Or doth He only wait to bless
'The new earth of His righteousness?'

Hark, hark the Heaven's soft reply
To Montenegro's battle cry,
To Servia struggling 'gainst the foe,
Bulgaria's haggard form of woe!

'Ye are my children, poor, oppressed,
And fighting for the crown of rest
That I have promised unto all,
Who on My Holy Name do call!

And ye have wandered from the truth,
My Gospel in its holy youth;
Yet though ye stand despised, alone,
What brother dare to cast a stone!

Was this the doctrine that I taught!
Is this the liberty I bought!
Is this the fruit My Gospel leaves,
My mercy in "a den of thieves!"

O souls, who suffer for My sake,
And still My Cross your burthen make,
By Adria's waters, Balkan's hills,
Bowed down beneath a load of ills:

Be brave, be true, your hour shall come,
My comfort to each shattered home,
My hour of triumph and of thine,
That dawned of old on Palestine;

That naught can hinder, naught can harm,
Nor friends so false, nor foes alarm—
I can protect, and I can save,
Can keep each soul My Father gave!

A. M.

DIED IN A PARIS CAFE, AUGUST, 1880.

WILL they miss her a moment in pleasure's mad whirl,
As they dance to their doom in the narrowing swirl!
Will they miss her, who charmed them—the brightest of all,
Who has answered before them the last dreaded call!

Will they miss her, whose beauty was all their delight,
And the grace of her presence the music of sight;
And who, struck to the earth in the pride of her power,
Shall remind them of sin and its terrible dower!

Will they miss her, the children of folly and flare,
The sweet siren who charmed with her loveliness rare;
Will they pause in a thrill of their passionate rave,
For a tear and a prayer o'er an actress's grave?

O frittered and fretful is the life of the age,
With its tinsels of pride and its fripperied stage ;
With its stimulant strength and its glaring of
 eve—
All too fevered to think and too weak to be-
 lieve !

O woman, created of our God in His love,
By thy grace and thy sweetness to lead us
 above,
But one life and one labour is offering meet,
Which both Mary and Magdalen found at His
 feet !

Egypt.

A SONNET.

O LAND where the light is of liquid gold,
And the air is a mystic dream of old—
A life like thy river so full and free,
A topic and type of Eternity!
From the day of the hoary priest of On
And Rameses' record of battles won,
Till the hour of the Infant Christ, Who found
A refuge, and made thee a holy ground!
Where His Saints in their need sought sweet
    repose,
And made thy deserts to bloom as the rose—
O Land of memories brightest and blest,
Where the mind and the heart alike find rest,
O waft ye a breath on this wintry day,
That shall meet my soul on its longing way!

Memories.

DEAR Friends, I would recall the time,
    That happy time of yore—
Those hours of blest companionship
    On Eastern Sea and Shore.

What better monument to mark
    Our friendship's genial rise,
Than Karnak's towers and columns vast—
    Eternal as the skies!

Than Memnon's mystery of form,
    Dendera's walls of pride,
And Philae's Isle of loveliness—
    The Monarch River's Bride!

The storied mass of Pyramid—
    Dear Friends, do you recall
That moonlit, musing hour within
    The Sphynx's desert hall!

How wrapt in voiceless awe we lay,
    Couched on the silent sand,
While Queenly Isis crowned with light
    The emblems of her land!

And O those days of pure delight,
    When floating down the stream,
Each living hour was ecstasy—
    One sweet and soothing dream!

O sunny hours too few, too far—
    Would life could ever be
A sailing down the summer stream
    Unto the summer sea!

Were such a wish for mortals weak,
    Were such a prayer of sin?
Ah, let but Eden's gates reope—
    Who would not enter in!

Then trod we Syria's sacred shore,
    With Sharon's roses fair:
And Olivet hath heard our hymn;
    Gethsemane our prayer!

O those dear hours on Sion's hill—
    Those happy hours of rest,
Thou holy City of my God
    Upon Thy Martyr breast!

How blest to dwell upon the soil
    That fed the Saviour's life—
To breathe the air beneath the skies,
    That cheered His toil and strife!

How sweet to kneel where He hath knelt,
    Where He hath preached and prayed;
To lay our heavy burden down
    Where His dear Form was laid!

What matters it that doubt enwraps
    The consecrated site!
The faith of pilgrim ages gives
    The heart's Divinest right!

O blessed hours in Jordan's vale;
    And Bethel's calm repose;
Samaria's bowers of nestling grace—
    The fig-tree and the rose!

Samaria's well, O hallowed spot!
    Who would not pause and pray—
And rest a while with Christ his Lord,
    Upon the weary way!

O sacred air that fanned His brow;
    Pure light that round Him played;
Sweet waters of His daily life;
    Blest mountains where He prayed!

God's world is beautiful indeed:
  That distant land of mine
Is fair—and yet, no love of earth
  Can make it Palestine!

'Tis true the wild flowers "blush unseen,"
  Where cities heard His cry—
The tangled bloom of wilderness
  Beneath the fadeless sky.

'Tis true Capernaum's voice is mute;
  Chorazin is no more;
Bethsaida's fisher-city sleeps
  Beneath the desert shore!

But O it is the land He loved,
  The region of His grace;
The earth reflects His loveliness;
  The heavens are His face!

Can you forget, dear Friends, that night
  On Tabor's beauteous brow,
When Palestine lay at our feet,
  Can you not see it now!

The sunset hour, the peerless view,
  All earth and sky one glow—
Judea's hills, fair Galilee
  To Hermon's crest of snow!

Can you forget, Beloved Friends,
    Gennesaret's holy sea—
The thrilling moment as we gazed
    On its lone purity!

And O that night upon the shore,
    That quiet eventide;
We sang the hymns of distant home
    And prayed Him 'to abide'—

Him, Whom those waters bore and Whom
    The Heavens cannot contain,
Who, as He went from earth, shall come
    Unto His Own again!

O sweet Esdraelon—can there be
    A fairer plain than thou,
With Carmel's Mount and Tabor's peak
    The jewels of thy brow!

O Land of God! O Light of Love,
    That smiles as sweet to-day,
And finds an answering thrill within
    The pilgrim hearts that pray!

The hills look down on Nazareth—
    The hills that looked of old,
And in their arms of living green
    The Saviour's Home enfold.

O holy hills that speak of God,
    That felt His Sinless Feet—
Infuse our souls with strength Divine,
    For such a Master meet!

Can you forget, dear Friends, that night
    On Akka's shadowy sand—
Our mournful march unto the sea,
    Our last of Holy Land!

Can you recall without a thrill
    That friendship tried and true,
Which still in shadow as in shine,
    Beneath God's blessing grew!

What shall we say of Lebanon,
    Reigning above the seas!
How shall we sing Damascus' bloom,
    Wooed by the desert breeze!

O Houri of the Orient waste,
    Fair genius of the sand—
No voice can tell thy loveliness,
    We bow to kiss thy hand!

Then Baalbec greets, in fallen pride,
    Lone Queen of Syria's wild,
Grand triumph of the ages' Art,
    Her lost, yet lovely child!

O City—lost to all but fame,
    Fallen yet full of grace,
Let Rome and Athens yield unto
    Thy still majestic face!

———

Again we sailed the summer seas,
    Amid the summer isles—
Refreshing green of Rhodian banks,
    And Cyprus wreathed with smiles.

And Smyrna's teeming marts of trade,
    With stranger contrast still—
The silent waste of Ephesus,
    Her ruin-crownéd hill!

O holy city of Saint John,
    Thy lesson is to me
Amid the saddest of them all—
    That pilgrim eyes could see!

The wild flowers bloom upon thy grave;
    Thy glory all is gone;
Diana's Temple sleeps beside
    The Churches of Saint John!

O Ruins few yet eloquent,
    Tell ye your tale again—
The story of the loving soul,
    Who spake of love to men

His Master's voice—to him who leaned
   Upon his Master's breast:
The first who proved his Saviour's word,
   "Come unto Me and rest!"

Again we sailed the silent seas,
   And bent the reverent head,
As Patmos' lonely isle recalled
   The Church's exiled head!

A little isle amid the seas—
   So desolate and bare,
Yet honoured once by the Divine,
   By Heaven's vision rare!

O day of stimulating light,
   When Athens charmed our gaze;
And Attic glory filled our souls—
   A happy, halcyon haze!

O Land of beauty and of grace—
   Land of the poet's song,
The soul that would thy praises sing,
   Must unto thee belong!

Alas, thou hast no Homers now,
   No Sapphos of the sea,
No heroes for thy Marathon,
   No leaders for thy free!

Thy freedom hath an Eastern ring,
    A toy by despots given—
It was not born in freedom's heart;
    It is no child of Heaven!

Be brave, be true, fair land of Greece;
    Thy suffering be thy grace—
Recall and live his words who once
    Preached to thy haughty race!

O day of mingled joy and pain,
    Our last on Eastern seas—
We passed the Orient's "golden gates,"
    Wooed by the Bosphorus breeze!

O vision of Aladdin's bliss,
    Bride of the Eastern main—
Happy the eyes that may behold
    Thy peerless site again!

O City of the saintly past,
    Profaned by Arab horde—
Shall evermore Sophia's dome
    Ring praises to the Lord!

Shall once again the bannered Cross
    Redeem those Eastern lands—
The Crescent wane till Islam's hosts
    Regain their desert sands?

O when shall He—the Christ of truth
  Return to bless His race,
The Region of His human birth,
  Of His Incarnate grace!

Come—as Thou camest, Prince of Life,
  In favoured Palestine!
Come on Thy Throne of Risen Might,
  Make every heart Thy shrine!

PART SECOND.

O happy hour we met again
  On Hudson's pleasant shore—
Those sunny hours of memory's sway—
  God grant us many more!

O dream of beauty and of bliss—
  O hours too sweet to last!
Reunion was as dear a joy
  As all the dreamy past!

We fought our pilgrim battles o'er,
  Our travellers' tales retold—
And Cairo greeted Assouan,
  The Nile her sands of gold!

The palm-tree waved on Hudson's bank,
  The lotus lulled our sense,
And all the Orient joy returned—
  As gracious, as intense!

We sang the hymns that make our land
  A second Palestine;
And felt the glow of Zion's sun,
  Gennesaret's voice Divine!

And Jordan sent her healing kiss,
  Bethel her gift of prayer,
And Nazareth her holy peace,
  Carmel her vision rare!

Again we slept by Lebanon,
  And in Damascus bowers;
Her living green refreshed our souls,
  And crowned the brimming hours!

Again we sailed the summer seas,
  Amid the happy isles—
The glad and gleaming waters round—
  The Orient's rippling smiles!

Again we trod the Morning lands,
  Rich in their storied past:
Each step a flood of memories
  And happier than the last!

O Lands that heard the voice of God,
  O Love that brings them near,
O Grace that led our feet so far,
  O Memories so dear!

'Twas meet, dear Friends, that in the Land,
  Where such a Friend abode,
Our hearts should feel some of that warmth,
  Which on His Followers flowed:

And O if these poor lines have brought
  But one deep, answering thrill,
Not unrewarded is their love,
  Which knows no change—nor will!

www.ingramcontent.com/pod-product-compliance
Lightning Source LLC
Chambersburg PA
CBHW020117170426
43199CB00009B/553